LOST RAILWAYS
OF
EAST YORKSHIRE

by

P. G. MASON

DEDICATION

To my stepfather, George Ebbs (1900-1980), born at Hexham, Northumberland. He was what every young boy wanted to be: an engine driver.

"Lost Railways of East Yorkshire" second edition. September 1992

ACKNOWLEDGEMENTS

My thanks to the following for their contribution in providing photographs and assistance, without which this book would not have been possible: British Rail, Yorkshire Post Newspapers, R. T. Porter, A. M. Ross, N. E. Pick, R. Howden, S. Lowe, Local History Unit, J. Clapham, A. J. Horne, W. C. Harding, N. Redmayne, K. E. Hartley, D. Cookson, M. L. Wilson, Humberside C.C., A. Jordan, C. A. Allenby, R. S. Holdsworth, S. Martin, and others.

Cover Picture — Kipling Cotes station today, which is better known as *'Grannies Attic'*. The track is owned by the local council and called *'Hudson's Way'*. It is used by ramblers who can walk from Market Weighton to Beverley un-hindered.

Copyright © 1990

No part of this book may be reproduced, stored in a retrieval system or transmitted in any form, or any means electronic, mechanical, photocopying, recording or otherwise without the prior permission of the Publisher and the Copyright holders.

Published and printed by Wolds Publications, Driffield, YO25 0HA
and typeset by
QuickSilver Typesetters, 4 Exchange Street, Driffield, YO25 7LJ

CONTENTS

	Introduction	7
Chapter One	This Man "Hudson"	9
Chapter Two	The Coming of a Railway	15
Chapter Three	Beverley-York Line	19
Chapter Four	Selby-Market Weighton-Driffield Line	25
Chapter Five	The Malton Dodger	29
Chapter Six	Hull-Withernsea Line	39
Chapter Seven	Hull-Hornsea Line	43
Chapter Eight	Hull and Barnsley Line	45
Chapter Nine	A Litte Railway at Spurn	51
Chapter Ten	The Derwent Valley Light Railway	55
Chapter Eleven	The North Holderness Light Railway	63

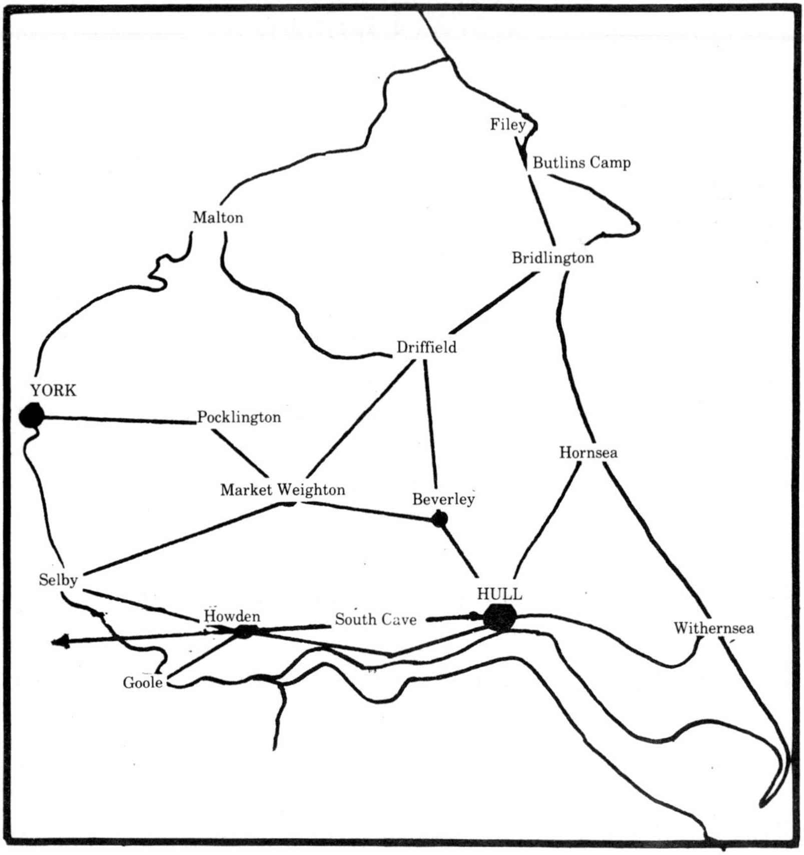

Map of East Yorkshire showing the principal railways.

The railway arrived in the East Riding of Yorkshire on July 22nd 1840. Since that time we have foolishly watched the demise of our great railway network. It is befitting that we remember those wonderful days — for many of us with sadness.

P.G.Mason.

Passengers No more!

North Grimston station

Wheldrake station (DVLR)

Stamford Bridge station (Beverley — York line)

Kipling Cotes station (Beverley — York line)

INTRODUCTION

The beginning of the railway age in Britain was marked by the Liverpool and Manchester line in 1830, but this was not the first railway. Many mines used narrow gauge railways to get the coal and ore out. Even as far back as 1550 a book was published illustrating the use of a narrow gauge line in the mines of Alsace. Also at the same time there were mine railways running in Central Europe. The flanged wheels and tracks were of wood.

The mine railways were an import from Germany. Many lines were in operation around the Newcastle area. Iron rails appeared in Cumberland in 1738, and in Surrey in 1801 the first public iron railway commenced.

In 1804, Richard Trevithick, a Cornish mining engineer, produced the first steam engine to run on rails. It hauled 10 tons of ore and 70 men at 5mph. Oystermouth near Swansea opened the first fare-paying passenger service in 1807. The motive power used for these lines was horses.

George Stephenson was the first man to build a public steam railway, at the request of the mine owners, in an effort to get coal to the wharves cheaply. He built twenty-seven miles of single track from Stockton to Darlington, but the line went beyond Darlington to Shildon in the Durham coalfield, and at the Stockton end of the line it ran right down to the quayside, a distance overall of thirty-eight miles.

Stephenson's line was operated by horse power, locomotives, and on the hilly parts of the line, steam winches were used. "Active" was his first locomotive, later to be re-named "Locomotion No. 1."

The line proved so successful it prompted the businessmen around Manchester to promote their own line in an effort to break the monopoly of the Manchester to Liverpool canal.

Plans for the railway met strong opposition from both canal and coaching interests as was the case with many railways that followed, hence the reason for railway companies buying the canals out and letting them fall into decay.

Stephenson was asked to survey and build the line, although he did have problems laying the track over the Chat Moss bog, which he overcame by laying it on brushwood and hurdles. He also met much opposition from those who wanted to run the trains by winch and cable in preference to locomotives.

Rainhill, just outside Liverpool, where the "trials" took place on October 6th 1829, made the promoters look again and finally succumb in favour of steam locomotives. There were plenty of competitors and thousands of spectators at the "trials"; even some from the lunatic fringe attended, but the more serious ones were George and Robert Stephenson in partnership with Henry Booth, Timothy Hackworth, the Swede, Captain John Ericsson, in partnership with John Braithwaite, Timothy Burstall from Scotland and Edward Bury from Liverpool.

At the end of the day it was Stephenson's "Rocket" that won the Rainhill Trials, and took the £500 prize money. It alone completed the twenty journeys on the two-mile track and fulfilled all the conditions laid down to pull 20 tons at a speed of not less than 10mph. The scenes were reminiscent of a race meeting with bets being laid, and opposition to the trials went on right up to the start, with many people still wanting to retain horse-drawn trains and cable power. It is ironical that even in those days technical change moved at such a pace as to make "Rocket" redundant within ten years. It was given to the London Science Museum in 1862.

Other entries were "Cycloped," which was disqualified at the start, when it was discovered to have a horse inside a frame, "San Pareil," "Perseverance" and the much favoured "Novelty," which reached extra fast speeds of 28mph, but could not pull a load, and kept breaking down. But this was no match for "Rocket," which maintained a speed of 15mph for 35 miles, and attained a top speed of 35mph.

7

Let us dwell for a moment on "Rocket." Stephenson built it at his Newcastle works and tested it out on the colliery railway at Killingworth. In comparison to the engines in use on the Stockton and Darlington Railway, "Rocket" was far superior. The boiler was the breakthrough. Prior to that most boilers were just tanks of water. Stephenson had designed a boiler with 25 copper tubes which the flames and hot gasses could pass freely through, thus, a dramatic increase in steam was produced. One of the main problems encountered was water leaking in at the joints of the tubes, but George's son, Robert, cured all the faults and announced that the engine was ready to carry out all the tests stipulated in the trials and much more. It was a confident Stephenson who went to Rainhill, dismantling and shipping his precious locomotive by sea to Liverpool.

He spent the next sixteen years, up to his retirement, developing, designing, helping, advising and building. Throughout the country there was not a line he was not consulted on. He died in 1848, the country a better place for having known George Stephenson.

The thirty-one miles of the Manchester to Liverpool line was opened by the Duke of Wellington on September 15th 1830, and contrary to expectations the line proved to be most successful for both goods and passengers. They deserted both canal and road travel for the speed and cheapness of the railway.

This inspired lines to be considered and built elsewhere. The railway had arrived. Railway companies mushroomed; over 250,000 navvies were employed in building railways at its peak in 1847. The equipment they used was very basic; in fact picks, shovels and wheelbarrows were the only tools most of them had. They lived in appalling conditions, usually alongside the tracks in squalid surroundings, and spread terror to the nearby villages on pay day. Despite all the problems and handicaps, the results were simply astonishing: within fifteen years lines had been opened between Birmingham and London, London and Southampton, the Grand Junction Railway, the Great Western and many other small lines. The Great Western did not adopt the standard gauge, but the problem was resolved by the Railways Act of 1921 when Parliament authorised over 120 companies to be merged into four, LNER, LMS, GWR and SR, the largest being the LMS.

It is interesting to note the return fare by stagecoach from London to Manchester in the 1830's was £3 10s (£3.50) and by rail 5/- (25p). Travel in those days could only be undertaken by the wealthy. People who had never travelled before flocked to the railway stations to experience this new-found freedom.

CHAPTER ONE

THIS MAN "HUDSON" (1800-1871)

(Mak all t'railways cum t'York)

The name of George Hudson will be popping up frequently as you read through this book, so it is understandable that you should wish to know a little about the man who had such a strong influence on the county of East Yorkshire. Although probably a little over-zealous, one has to give credit and admire this man, who did so much in bringing a new way of life for the many people who had never ventured beyond their village. To even begin to write a condensed article about him is a task in itself. He achieved so much in such a small space of time. George rose rapidly to such great heights and with the same speed fell to such great depths.

Indeed, had he carried on his business activities today, as he did in the past, he would surely have gone to prison for many years.

George Hudson was born at the Wolds village of Howsham, between Stamford Bridge and Malton, on March 10th 1800. He was the fifth son of John Hudson, who farmed the area. George was only eight when his father died, leaving him £10,000. The farm was divided up amongst the eldest sons. An entry in the Howsham poor book read "6th April 1815 to 6th April 1816 received of George Hudson for Bastardy 12/6d."

He was apprenticed to Nicholson and Bell, who were drapers and silk mercers in College Street, York. At twenty-one he married Nicholson's daughter, Elizabeth, who was five years his senior and worked in the shop alongside George. He later became a partner in the firm. Always a staunch Tory and Methodist, he preached quite often at the local halls.

In 1827, Hudson's great uncle, Mathew Botterill, died leaving George a fortune, thirty thousand pounds in cash, together with land at Huntington and Osbaldwick, making George one of the richest men in York. How he came by such wealth has always been viewed with suspicion. Mathew Botterill was a gentleman with an address in Monkgate, who gave a lot of support to William Wilberforce MP. The story goes that George was at the old man's bedside and, although never proven, the will was altered within the last few days of him dying. Evidence suggests that the will was, in fact, altered. Botterill died on May 25th. The will was dated April 21st and George Hudson was named sole executor.

George took control of the Tory party in York and the council. He did in fact hold the post of Lord Mayor twice. This in itself was manoeuvred by his fellow party members. They all liked George. He was famous for throwing lavish banquets at the drop of a hat. Any event would be an excuse to wine and dine with no expense spared.

He became the Tory party front bench spokesman in the House of Commons responsible for the railways and the many bills.

It was not considered illegal to buy votes at elections, and up to 1835, when a bill was passed in Parliament for government reform, this was the way most MPs got elected.

Whilst trade was booming in many West Riding towns like Bradford, Leeds and Halifax, York was in the doldrums. Hudson and his cronies were envious of this situation and wanted the same for their city. The main problem was the price of coal and its transportation. If coal could be got down in price, then York too could once more become an industrial centre.

The Ouse was the main artery of trade up to the railways coming, and an effort to improve this navigation with the main objective of reducing the cost of coal was, indeed, the intention but the money was spent unwisely. In December 1835, Hudson and a group of businessmen gathered at the Tomlinson Hotel in York with a view to taking a railway into York. The line would run from York to South Milford where a junction with the Leeds to Selby line was made. In true Hudson style, a lavish banquet was laid on and that was the birth of the York and North Midland Railway (YNMR).

In the early days of Victoria, the coming of the railways, an iron road and new motive power, was viewed with awe. It changed people's lives, the fast communication which, prior to the railways, had been slow and uncomfortable in a horse and coach and took days, now took a few hours. A revolution had occurred: even one small branch line to a small community changed their lives drastically.

Steam engines, railway stations, viaducts, tunnels, cuttings, all new and exciting, had a magic of their own. Speed and all the things associated with it, travel, amusement, education and health, all this would enrich society, and Hudson perceived it all. He had visions of what could and would be.

It was the railway mania of the 1830's and 40's that created lines that were to be inefficient in the years to follow, lines that did not really go anywhere.

Scrayingham Church and grave where Hudson was buried.

Hudson was a great friend of George Stephenson. Both men knew that, for the railways to be successful, amalgamation between competing lines was essential to prevent waste and reduce costs. This would result in a better service to the public.

He bought up land, mainly to use as pawns in the railway game of obstructing his competitors as well as elevating his family up the social ladder. He had estates at Baldersby Park and Londesborough Hall as well as having interests in Whitby and Scarborough, and it was indeed thanks to Hudson that these resorts grew to what they are today.

At the height of his power he controlled a vast network of enterprises. Other great industrialists of that time pale into insignificance beside him for pure energy and the capacity to simultaneously direct many complex enterprises. The slow-moving world of 1845 with no telephones, dictating machines or typewriters, cars or planes, was amazed at the speed in which he got things done. He was the man who engineered a controlled monopoly of railway management, one of the few businessmen who could drop into today's business world with no problem.

Hudson's energies flowed into railways, docks, banking and finance, land and property, together with his local and national politics. At the height of his career he was in control of four large railway systems, some fifteen hundred miles of track out of a total of five thousand miles of railway in England, plus the construction of docks at Sunderland, Monk Wearmouth and Hull. He was also a principal shareholder in a glassworks at South Shields which supplied glass to his stations as well as being in iron which supplied rails for the track.

He was the founder and chairman of the York Union Bank and had a strong influence on the stock exchange. All manner of person was found to be speculating in shares and it is hard to believe the influence the railways had over people. A return called for by Parliament to show the number of persons who had subscribed over £2,000 in the railways included some 900 lawyers, 364 bankers, 237 clergymen and 157 MPs, besides noblemen, merchants and manufacturers. Even the Brontë sisters of Haworth bought shares. Such was the enthusiasm that it lead to many businesses being neglected. One would call at a shop or office to be met with "Gone to the city." All rule and order was upset by the general epidemic and friendships were cast aside. At the Royal Exchange each morning people poured in from the suburbs by coach and horse-drawn omnibus. Share markets were set up in York and Leeds. The mania continued to rage so long as the money remained cheap. People borrowed for their deposits, the politicians became alarmed at the drain on the country's resources into the railways. The nation had gone mad, "The Times" warned against further speculation and even the chairmen of some of the railway companies became terrified, as "bubble" projects for new and competing lines multiplied each week.

The Bank of England decided in October that it had to raise its rate of interest; from enthusiasm the country went to panic, shares fell overnight in value, many projects were dropped and applications fell away, calls were not met and loans were demanded for repayment.

During these months Hudson was in the north of England but had decided that he must move down to London. In a blaze of glory he left York to take up his seat in Parliament, where they eagerly awaited his first speech. He became a millionaire, mixed with the cream of society and had regular meetings with the Duke of Wellington.

In 1846 Hudson returned to the north to find the shares in the Midland railway fast declining on the stock market. Other lines began to fall. Even the YNMR shares were not what they were. This, however, did not sour his homecoming; indeed, he had the Freedom of York conferred on him.

The amalgamation of lines north of York into a single great company was the first step and was accomplished in two stages and called the Great North of England Railway.

11

It was about this time that Hudson, with more grand plans for even more railways, met with opposition from the Government, requiring vast amounts of capital for what his enemies considered unsound schemes, and sacrificing the interest of his investors to the greed of speculators. By juggling money and robbing Peter to pay Paul he met both his creditors and paid out his shareholders. He would transfer large amounts of money from one company to another to meet dividends. He admitted in 1848 that they were struggling with many new lines. In short Hudson had over-reached himself and would have done better to have slowed down the pace of his railway building. He blamed all manner of things for their plight. These were unpleasant words to come from the Railway King, words that were repeated to the Midland, as well as the York, Newcastle and Berwick shareholders. However, he did manage to pay a dividend of seven and nine per cent, and it was felt that things would improve. Unfortunately, during 1848 the incalculable occurred; revolution, beginning in February with France and spreading through Germany, Austria, Italy and Poland, and even into Britain the shock was felt, through a sudden resurgence of Chartism during March and April, and an outbreak of unrest in Ireland.

Far from improving things, business grew steadily worse and this proved fatal for Hudson. His liabilities could only be met by an increase in traffic. Within twelve months his empire began to crumble, but besides the revolution other lesser pieces of misfortune contributed to increase his decline.

In himself he was not a well man, probably due to the high state of living over the years, and the speed at which he lived his life together with the many miles of travelling. Working late at night and spending many hours in the stuffy atmosphere of the House of Commons, nature was taking its revenge. In April 1848, he had to take to his bed with a digestive disorder which in later life affected and weakened his heart. This caused the occurrence of angina, and meant a slowing down of his public life. At the same time his unprofitable Eastern Counties Railway had exhausted its money supply and a dividend of eight shillings on a twenty pound share was announced. Gloom also prevailed at a meeting of the YNMR and the York and Berwick company as a reduced dividend was issued. Attacks were levied at him from a pamphlet published by Arthur Smith, exposing financial weakness, which Hudson refused to comment on, and rumours were rife that he was about to retire.

Hudson was sincere in his devotion to the YNMR, whose accounts he had always kept with less manipulation that those of other companies. Indeed, with all the malpractices that he had taken part in, he always claimed that he did it in the interest of the company and never made a penny from it. He was never prosecuted for any offences. In order to pay even a reduced dividend meant the use of unorthodox accountancy, and borrowing from various banks for various companies. The problem was meeting the repayment, which left each company with very little working capital. There was a general decline in share values and investors were pressing for an investigation into the true state of their property, wanting all the facts and figures as to earnings and expenditure. At this critical moment, Hudson was again taken ill. The Railway King's prestige was beginning to sink even in York, with unfulfilled promises and no more capital available. The end had come; creditors clamoured for their money and duped shareholders were near to rebellion.

There had also been some dubious dealings in a large number of shares of some small denomination which had been bought by the company at an inflated rate. In fact the shares had never ever been worth more than twenty-one pounds, and now here they were being bought at twenty-three pounds ten shillings, double their present value. A certain Robert Prance posed the

Hudson's house at Howsham.

THESE GRAVES WERE RENOVATED IN 1935
BY MEMBERS OF THE HUDSON FAMILY, AND A
FEW ADMIRERS OF GEO. HUDSON, KNOWN AS
THE RAILWAY KING AND SON OF THE ABOVE
JOHN & ELIZABETH HUDSON.

question to Hudson that, as only a few of the shares were held by the public, some individual had made quite a profit on the deal.

This was Hudson's big mistake, a fatal and irretrievable false step. He stammered out that he had owned 2,800 of the shares, and that perhaps there had been a slight overcharge, for which he tried to put the blame onto a fellow director. He tried to talk his way out of the situation, and indeed years earlier he would have succeeded, but not any more. His audience viewed things in a different light; a few were prepared to take a refund with interest, but Prance would not hear of it. "Here we have a matter of reputation," and insisted upon a committee to investigate the whole sordid affair. The meeting broke up in turmoil with rumours flying from one end of York to the other. The enquiry inevitably led to more revelations and disclosure even more disastrous and more startling, not only the misappropriation of shares but publication of false balance sheets and manipulation of accounts, declaring and paying dividends from borrowed money and other railway stock. The fact that he had been found out and questioned about it amazed Hudson.

The whole investigation and the findings cannot be gone into but the Railway King now knew that his whole political career was in peril. From being adulated and courted by all, his name became overnight a by-word and a mockery amongst some of his most faithful. There were calls for Hudson to be prosecuted, but it was felt that, had he been prosecuted, it could end up placing many other people in a very dangerous position.

The demise of Hudson must be considered as sad and, possibly, foolish on his side. After failing to win a seat in the election at Sunderland he realised that it was the end of his career. He went into exile, fearing that if he stayed in England he might end up in prison. He travelled between the channel ports living in cheap hotels growing poorer and shabbier. Finally his money ran out. He was seen by Charles Dickens on one occasion, whilst stepping on to the boat at Boulogne to Folkestone, noting what a pitiful sight he was.

In 1865 Hudson returned to Whitby. To his delight he found things had changed and people had forgotten about his past errors. Many regarded him as a victim of persecution by his creditors. Just forty-eight hours before the election Hudson was arrested for debt. He was held in York town prison. Three months later he was released, his creditors knowing they would get nothing out of him.

He settled in London. His health failing, a few of his friends rallied round and decided to free him from his debts. £4,800 was raised to buy him an annuity of £600. He began to hold up his head once more and was even re-elected chairman of the smoking room at the Carlton Club.

In 1871 he paid a visit to his birthplace (Howsham) but illness once more came upon him, and between attacks of angina he managed to travel back to London. On December 14th 1871 he died. Six days later his body was transported from London to York via the Midland line, and at 9.30am the funeral procession made its way through York, simple and unostentatious by Hudson's request.

The Minster and other church bells tolled, tradesman closed their shutters and people lined the streets. The hearse, on leaving the city, entered the Derwent valley and continued on to the Wolds. George was back home, resting in the tiny peaceful village churchyard at Scrayingham, far from the lifestyle he had once enjoyed.

Hudson once declared that his happiest days had been serving behind the shop counter, and the worst thing was inheriting the fortune from his Great Uncle Botterill which had led him into the railways and misfortune.

CHAPTER TWO
THE COMING OF A RAILWAY

Hull had always been a growing port from as far back as the Middle Ages, but its growth was brought about more rapidly by the long wars with France (1793-1815). It was the tendencies of Governments to make more use of northerly ports in time of war. In addition to that the Humber was also a large naval base.

It was because of this expansion at the Humber ports that more space was required and there arose the necessity to build more docks. Between 1778 and 1829 three docks replaced the ditch and town fortifications in what is now the Queen's Gardens in the centre of the city.

Adding to the trade from foreign ports, Hull also shared in the prosperity that was to come from the growth of industry in the West Riding and the Midlands, Yorkshire's wool products, steel and coal being exported out of the country, and imports of bar iron and wool coming in through the Humber port, and thence via the rivers Ouse and Trent.

Hull, therefore, was just as involved in the Industrial Revolution as were such places as Sheffield, Manchester, Leeds and Birmingham. It was the unlimited possibilities that attracted developers like Hudson to look more closely into the building of a railroad linking Hull to the West.

With the Knottingley-Goole canal and a new port at Goole under construction in the 1820's, there was a feeling of great urgency for a line to be built and opened as soon as possible.

The plans for a Leeds-Selby-Hull railway did not materialise as quickly as would have been liked, and it was not until 1840 that the Hull-Selby section of the line was completed, and a full service began to operate. Plans for the line were laid as early as 1825 but held back because of the fear of the competition from the steamers that run up the Ouse.

In 1824, The Hull and Leeds Railroad Company was formed and in 1825 Benjamin Gott, a well-known Leeds cloth manufacturer, asked George Stephenson to survey a route for a proposed railway between Leeds and Selby. This was four years before "Rocket" beat off all competitors at the Rainhill trials. On surveying the route, Stephenson was not happy with the gradients, and was not sure that such a line, relying on locomotive power alone, could be worked without the addition of horses and stationary engines for winching. Gott was not satisfied with Stephenson's proposals, so he asked for a second opinion, and in 1829 James Walker from London was invited to cast his expert eye over the terrain. Walker altered the route slightly and was quite convinced that the line could be worked throughout by locomotives. The total cost of building would be £200,000.

On June 1st 1830, an Act of Parliament was obtained, following much opposition by the Aire and Calder Navigation Company, who up until this time had monopolised all the trade.

There were many Hull and East Yorkshire businessmen financially involved in the venture. Their sole purpose was to bring a railway to Hull as quickly as possible to speed up the trade with the West Riding.

The Leeds and Selby part of the line was opened up to traffic on September 22nd 1834, but the line proved to be a failure. A local Selby man, James Audus, did his best to promote the line, even introducing steam packets to connect passengers with Hull. It was here that one of the first packets to be built completely of iron was launched in 1835.

15

The problem that arose with the rail/boat travel system was the difficulty in maintaining a punctual service. The timetables had to be staggered to meet the tide times of the Ouse and the Humber.

The decline of the trade from 1836 to 1840 resulted in the line being let to Hudson's growing York and North Midland Company at a cost of £17,000 per year, only to be bought out by them four years later for the sum of £340,000.

The merchants in and around Hull at that time were most disappointed at the failure to extend the line beyond Selby. The advantages of a through rail link were apparent and the potential enormous. There was also the growing fear that Goole would take advantage of this situation, and with the opening of the Goole-Knottingley canal in 1826 it soon came to the fore as a rapidly growing port, even winning foreign trade.

Goole began to show signs of great prosperity and took a lion's share of the Humber trade, with rumours some four years later that a line from Barnsley to Goole was being suggested, giving the port a firm hold in the coal-exporting trade.

In the 1830's there were certain parties at the coastal resorts of Bridlington and Scarborough viewing the railways with great favour, and a whole new wealth of people from the West Riding wishing to visit the seaside. This, however, did not meet with the approval of the merchants around Hull. The planned route of the line from York was to take in Pocklington, Driffield and then go on to Bridlington, which would connect with a line between York and Leeds. There were also plans to modernise and extend harbour facilities at Bridlington and develop the town as a major fishing port to serve the West Riding market.

A gentleman by the name of John Exley, who worked for the Customs and Excise at Hull, played a major role in alerting the public to the benefits that would be derived from a Selby to Hull line. He worked out the economics and presented a favourable projection together with a ten per cent dividend. With support from local newspapers, two Hull bankers, George Liddell and James Henwood, took the initiative in raising £20,000, which was required by Parliament. The rest of the money was not so forthcoming. The usual arguments were raised by the landowners to the west of the city whose land the railway would have to pass over.

The line was planned to take in Welton, North and South Cave, but the Raikes family of Welton were not keen on the idea at all. Eventually they were offered a £10,000 sweetener providing there was no station on the estate. The station was built at Brough and the route changed; so, instead of serving North and South Cave, the line went from Brough dead straight for eighteen miles (the longest straight stretch of line in the country). Raising the rest of the capital was fraught with problems, the local area contributing £155,000. By 1836 investment became much easier; £90,000 came from the London area and £20,000 from Liverpool.

Competition from the steam packets did not seem the threat it had first appeared, as the opening of the Leeds-Selby line had proved with the Aire and Calder Navigation, forcing them to reduce their freight charges from 7/- to 2/3 per ton, a major reduction.

It was this kind of impact the Leeds-Selby had had that changed the thinking about the Selby-Hull line, it being able to offer a more reliable and punctual service than the rivers and canals ever could, with their reliance on tides and the constant fears of running aground on the ever-shifting sands of the Humber.

It must be remembered that Selby as a railway terminal and port held a prominent position up to 1826. But, with the opening of the Knottingley-Goole canal, the older Selby canal was by-passed, and with the forthcoming line it would only be an intermediate station between Leeds and Hull. This did not look too favourable for Selby. However, the promoters of the line felt that trade to Selby would be increased. With the proposals for a

16

line from York to London, Selby would be in the unique position of being at the crossroads of these two great railways.

The Hon. Edward Robert, Lord Petre, owned the ferry rights over the Ouse at Selby and was proprietor of the Bridge of 1792. He, together with the Mayor, aldermen and councillors of York, Robert Raikes of Welton, George Earle, a merchant from Hull (possibly Earles Cement), and trustees of the Market Weighton-Selby turnpike, all opposed the line. After many minor amendments, the bill received Royal Assent on June 21st 1836. At last, a line through to Hull was becoming a reality.

Four years later, on Wednesday, July 1st 1840, the Selby to Hull line held its opening ceremony. The following day, Thursday July 2nd, it opened to the public.

The Hull station was in Railway Street, close to what is now the Hull Mariner. Workshops and part of the station were in Kingston Street. Eight years later passenger traffic was moved to a new more centrally situated home, Paragon Station, which opened on May 8th 1848.

The standard gauge set for railways was four feet eight and a half inches, but the gauge on the Hull-Selby was half an inch wider to allow more play on the wheel flanges.

The opening ceremony was marred by bad weather which resulted in the cancellation of the procession around the town. However, this did not deter some. The Manchester Unity of Oddfellows, together with their Hull friends, paraded the area accompanied by several bands. Mr. Levitt and his musicians then performed a number of suitable tunes whilst travelling towards Selby. On arrival, visitors were treated to a banquet in the company's warehouse, where fifteen tables had been laid out with 750 dishes.

The first train left Hull at 12.10pm to mark the official opening, passing through Hessle at 12.26pm to a great roar from the crowds lining the track, and arriving in Selby at 2.15pm.

Locomotives on the line were "Prince," "Kingston," "Selby," "Andrew Marvel" and "Exley" (named after John Exley). The "Prince" was loaned by the Leeds-Selby company for the day.

As had been forecast, the new line was a great success with passengers for the first week totalling four and a half thousand. This meant a great loss for, and the final demise of, the river steamers. Five weeks after the line had been opened a derailment at Wressle caused the death of five passengers and several people were injured, causing a drop in receipts, but the company placed the blame on the lack of Sunday travel.

The early days of the line were well patronised. Trade fell off during the slump of 1841-42, but a new boom began which grew to fever pitch up to 1845, then once more trade fell away sharply as the bubble burst, but again during 1846 things began to recover.

Those early unstable years of the railways occurred mainly due to over-investment and falling interest rates. For a time it seemed much better to have any idle money invested in the growing railways with high returns, rather than sitting in a bank where the return on one's capital was much lower. This situation, however, encouraged irresponsible trading, what we would call the "fast buck." This did not help to stabilise the situation. Our own county did not escape from these financial ills, and many ideas were put forward which did not materialise. If they had, we would most certainly have had a different face on the railways of East Yorkshire than that we know today.

HULL AND SELBY, OR HULL AND LEEDS JUNCTION, RAILWAY.
OPENING OF THE LINE
FOR PASSENGERS AND PARCELS ONLY,
ON THURSDAY, JULY THE 2nd, 1840.

THE Public are respectfully informed that this RAILWAY IS OPENED THROUGHOUT from HULL to the JUNCTION with the LEEDS and SELBY RAILWAY, at Selby, for the Carriage of PASSENGERS and PARCELS, presenting a direct Railway Conveyance from Hull to Selby, Leeds, and York, without change of Carriage.

TRAINS WITH PASSENGERS WILL START FROM HULL AS UNDER:

AT SEVEN O'CLOCK, A.M. | AT THREE O'CLOCK, P.M.
AT TEN O'CLOCK, A.M. | AT SIX O'CLOCK, P.M.

ON SUNDAYS, AT SEVEN O'CLOCK, A.M., AND SIX O'CLOCK, P.M.

The Trains from LEEDS and YORK will depart from those Places at the same Hours, with the exception of the Evening Trains, which will leave Leeds and York at SEVEN O'CLOCK, in order that the Passengers leaving London at Nine o'Clock in the Morning may arrive in Hull at Half-past Nine o'Clock the same Evening. The Trains will leave YORK and LEEDS on SUNDAY EVENINGS at SIX O'CLOCK.

Passengers and Parcels may be Booked through at the Leeds, York, and Hull Stations. Arrangements have been made for forwarding Passengers to Sheffield, Derby, Birmingham, London, &c., by the Trains which leave Hull at Seven and Ten A.M.

There are no Trains from Hull at 11 A.M. and 5 15 P.M. as Advertised by the North Midland and Midland Counties Railway Companies, and owing to an alteration just made by those Companies, Passengers cannot at present be forwarded from Hull to London by the Train at 3 P.M.

THE FARES TO BE CHARGED ARE AS UNDER:

First Class.   *Second Class.*   *Third Class.*

Hull to Selby............4s. 6d..............4s. 0d..... ....2s. 6d.
Hull to York ....8s. 0d..............6s. 6d............ .....4s. 6d.
Hull to Leeds............8s. 0d......6s. 6d. .... 4s. 6d.

No Fees are allowed to be taken by the Guards, Porters, or any other Servants of the Company.

The Trains, both up and down will call at the Stations on the Line, viz.:—Hessle, Ferriby, Brough, Staddlethorpe, Eastrington, Howden, and Cliff.

Arrangements for conveying Goods, Cattle, Sheep, &c., will be completed in a short time, of which due Notice will be given.   By Order,

GEORGE LOCKING, Secretary.

Railway Office, Hull, July 3rd, 1840.

Advertisement from the Hull Advertiser, 10th July, 1840

CHAPTER THREE
BEVERLEY-YORK LINE (1847-1965)

Probably from all the rail closures that were implemented by Beeching when reshaping the railways, the Beverley to York was certainly one railway, although never admitted, whose closure must have been a drastic mistake. Why, in the first place, this line was even considered, together with the haste in which it was closed, will never be fully understood. One cannot put all the blame on to the Tory Government, with a general election looming, promises to halt rail closures and inspect lines with a little more scrutiny only served to prolong the closing for a short time, and was purely an election ploy by the Labour Government.

In the days of mass branch line closures, many people felt that their line should not be closed through personal or even selfish reasons, but if lines were not being sufficiently used or running at great losses it was inevitable that the line would eventually be closed. This became a very debatable subject, with the fors against rail closures of any kind using the argument that railways throughout the world lose money, and they provide a public service.

The line closed on November 29th 1965. I would like to endorse a quote by Stephen Chapman in his book "Hudson's Way": "An event in railway history which should never have been allowed to happen."

Most of the line was built in the Wolds area, and the fact that Market Weighton was a very busy junction for both the Beverley to York and the Selby to Driffield did not seem to enter into the consideration when closures were discussed. It was also backed by the Railway King himself, George Hudson.

The railway, although mentioned as the York to Beverley and bisected by the Yorkshire Wolds, went through to Hull, connecting north of Beverley with the Hull-Bridlington line.

Hull was an expanding port and Hudson's YNMR (York and North Midlands Railway) saw great potential with a link with York.

In the early 1800's lines were opened at the drop of a hat, and although an Act of Parliament had to be passed, things moved very quickly in those days where the railways were concerned. People would scan the local papers looking for any new railway to invest their money in. Indeed, there was never any shortage of investors, and railways sprang up all over the place.

The first section from York to Market Weighton opened in 1847, but Hudson knew that, without the Beverley link, the line could never be really viable. Due to the stubbornness of local landowners and the difficult terrain it was a further seventeen years before the line reached Beverley.

Closing the line was certainly detrimental to the communities that lived alongside it. If ever a railway was justified and still is, it was this one. Modernisation, which almost happened, would have made the Beverley-York profitable with great prospects for an even better future. With the growth in population and light industries at Market Weighton, Pocklington and Stamford Bridge, not to mention villages that have grown in population (one has only to look at Cherry Burton), and the farming communities, who in latter years have shipped enormous quantities of grain and produce, by overcrowded and narrow roads, a better transport system was obviously needed.

19

Fangfoss station.

Market Weighton station.

The bus services that were going to solve the problem were proved to be inadequate, unreliable, slow and expensive. Most of these services too are gone, and fortunately for rural areas the deregulation of the bus companies has meant the introduction of small community buses, although travellers wishing to go to York from Hull must now make the trip via Selby.

The York-Beverley line dates back to 1865, but as far back as 1845 in the days of railway mania the Manchester-Leeds Railway wanted to break the monopoly held by Hudson and his York and North Midland Railway. He held on to routes through to Hull with his own line, York, Hull and East Riding Railway. Hudson tried many times to buy the Manchester and Leeds off, but only partially succeeded. In fact it ended up with him parting with half his shares of the one hundred per cent lease he held on the Hull-Selby Junction Railway, giving the Manchester-Leeds a direct access to Hull, an unwise move for a clever and shrewd operator.

This situation placed Hudson and his YNMR under an obligation to build a line from York through to Hull, and it was at this time when the Hull to Barnsley Railway were showing interest with a line to the West Riding coal fields.

Hudson got in first with his plans to build a line from Selby to Driffield, thus cutting right across the proposed Hull-Barnsley line. At that time it was of no consequence as the H&B failed in Parliament to get approval for the line, and Hudson could only take his line as far as Market Weighton.

Many options were considered at the time, one being a line from York to Brough, and then along the Selby-Hull section. Eventually they settled for York to Beverley via Market Weighton. Seven weeks later the Railways Act was passed and three years were allowed for them to acquire the land and five years to complete the building work.

On August 12th 1846, the line from Bootham to Market Weighton was staked out and September 30th 1847 was the date set for completion. On October 3rd 1847, trains were running just three days over the scheduled time. Because of petty wrangling the Selby-Market Weighton line was delayed and did not officially open until August 1st 1848. All building work on both lines then stopped, leaving Market Weighton as the terminus, and so it remained for a further seventeen years before the route through to Beverley was completed. Reasons for the delay were blamed on Lord Hotham of Dalton for the conditions he forced upon the company. Most of the line from Market Weighton passed over his estate. Without this section of line being completed the rest of the line was pointless, as was stated when plans for the line were first mooted.

This halt in the work caused many local people to raise petitions. A mandamus (a writ issued by a superior court) compelling the YNMR to build the line was sought, but the YNMR were under no obligation to finish the line as the period for compulsory purchase had run out.

From York the line ran over many roads and tracks, and for a distance of twenty-two miles there were twenty-two level crossings, one of the reasons put forward a century later for the line's downfall. There were many accidents with farm animals straying on to the tracks.

Although the line terminated at Market Weighton, surprisingly, it still proved profitable, but further growth was stunted. Hudson even had his own private station built at Londesborough Hall, passing at the lower end of an avenue of trees, which can still be seen today.

On July 31st 1854, the North Eastern Railway company was formed which took in the Beverley-York and, because of the name similarities on some of the stations, they changed the names so as not to cause confusion. Huntington (Huntingdon) became Earswick, Stockton became Warthill. Gate Helmsley changed its name to Holtby in 1872 and was closed on September 11th 1939.

21

The first continental lifting barriers installed in Britain for B.R. at Warthill (Beverley-York line).

The newly formed North Eastern soon found itself besieged for the rail link to Hull to be completed, and in 1856 the Mayor of Hull pressed for the York-Brough scheme to be reconsidered. The vicar of South Cave, the Reverend E. W. Stillingfleet, was not very happy about it, stating: "Had we a railway, I have little doubt that bad would be made much worse. The scum of Hull would make South Cave a place for Sunday revels."

In 1860 NER decided to go ahead with the Beverley connection despite the tough bargaining laid down by Lord Hotham. Although process was slow eventually in September 1862 work began. One of Lord Hotham's conditions was that a station should be built to serve his estate, and although NER suggested Goodmanham, Lord Hotham found this to be not acceptable and suggested one at Kipling Cotes, a remote sight for passengers alighting, with no visible sign of habitation apart from a couple of distant farms and cottages set in the rolling hills.

Another condition laid down by Lord Hotham was that no trains would be allowed to run on a Sunday, and for the full life of the line I can never remember this condition ever being lifted. The terrain across the Wolds made working difficult and it took three years to cover the ten miles with a single track to Beverley. The line finally opened on May 1st 1865. After leaving York, the train sped through the Vale of York, crossing the River Derwent at Stamford Bridge over a ninety-foot high viaduct, which can still be seen today, then skirting the foot of the Wolds to Pocklington before reaching Market Weighton and preparing itself for the heavy slog up and over the Wolds to Cherry Burton and then on to Beverley.

Market Weighton was an extremely busy junction and in summer it also coped with heavy holiday traffic to Bridlington and Butlins at Filey which in its heyday had its own station, *(opened in 1947 closed 1977)* but in the 60's, when more people became car owners, traffic declined on all railways, and

Stamford Bridge station.

closures for the less profitable loomed. It was decided to spend £83,000 on modernisation (continental barriers, line to be made single track with loops) and some stations closed down. In January 1961, approval was given and the relay rooms were to be completed by 1962. The delivery of equipment started straight away. One can imagine the shock when, in 1962, Beeching singled out the Beverley-York line for closure. At that time it was making £6,000 per year profit, with the possibility of higher profits after modernisation. Somehow Beeching's figures were not quite the same. He said closing the line would result in a saving of £43,000. Warthill, Fangfoss and Cherry Burton were closed from January 5th 1959 and in 1962 Londesborough station closed and the CTC scheme halted. There was still hope that the line would be saved with the impending general election and Labour promises "that all lines would be reviewed before closed down," but the new transport minister, Barbara Castle, against all the protests and advice, promptly sanctioned the death of the Beverley to York and hammered the final nail in the coffin. The line was to close on October 8th 1965, but was given a stay of execution to enable bus services to be organised. Sadly services ceased on the 29th November 1965.

Despair fell on the whole community. Many people in the Wolds area had actually voted for the Labour Government, thinking they were saving their railway. Prime Minister Wilson was lobbied and sanctions were threatened against BR. People claimed the figures had been falsified or some incompetent typist had made a typing error. Whatever the reason, and we may never know the truth, British Rail and the Government were not interested.

Several old stations were converted into dwellings, others pulled down. Houses have been built on parts of the old line, and the once busy Market Weighton station was sold to the North Wolds Council for £373,000. The section between Market Weighton and Beverley has now been turned into a nature trail, and aptly named Hudson's Way. I wonder what George would have made of Beeching had he been alive to fight the closure. Having read what kind of man Hudson was, I doubt if even Barbara Castle dared have closed it.

Earswick station.

Kipling Cotes station

CHAPTER FOUR
SELBY -MARKET WEIGHTON- DRIFFIELD LINE

The development by Hudson of a line from Selby to Market Weighton did not reach its full potential until the line was extended from Market Weighton over the Wolds to Driffield by the Scarborough, Bridlington and West Junction Railway Company, opening on 18th April 1890. This was only a freight service but a fortnight later passenger services commenced, thus linking the industrial West Riding to the east coast resorts of Bridlington, Filey and Scarborough in a direct route, without the need of going via Hull.

The completion of this line, together with the York-Beverley railway, placed Market Weighton in a very strategic position. It was at the very crossroads, making this small market town a bustling hive of activity. The line from Selby to Market Weighton opened on August 1st 1848. Initially it was single track, and the cost of building the line was £156,000. The line was later to be doubled when taken over by North Eastern Railways.

It would be worth mentioning at this point, that in addition to the cost in building the lines in East Yorkshire, money had to be set aside to buy people off and get rid of any opposition. The main opponents to the railways were the owners of the canals. Pocklington, which was in fact losing money, was purchased for £18,000. Leven, Market Weighton and Holme canal (also known as Sir Edward Vavasour's Canal) had to be bought out. The latter in fact was never taken over. Although they did not cease to operate, money was never forthcoming towards their upkeep, and gradually through decline and competition and the speed of delivery from the railways, they gradually silted up and ceased to operate.

The line from Selby to Market Weighton in the early days could not be classed as a big money spinner. With an average of four trains a day in each direction, it did a lot for the rural communities along the line, making life much easier. It enabled them to get their goods and cattle to market at Selby far more quickly than in the past, when the only mode of transport was horse and cart.

The first station out of Selby was at Cliff Common, also the terminus of the DVLR, then on to Bubwith, Foggathorpe and Market Weighton.

From Market Weighton the train had to climb for three and a half miles up Enthorpe Bank, a gradient of 1 in 100. Most trains did manage without assistance, but some of the passenger excursion trains were double headed.

From running over the flat farmlands of the Derwent Valley to Market Weighton, the contrast changed dramatically as the trains climbed up on to the high chalk hills, through isolated cuttings and small bridges and breathtaking beauty of the Yorkshire Wolds. Population on the section to Middleton on the Wolds was a little sparse, just farms dotted here and there, and although a station was planned for Goodmanham, one was never built. Instead, Lord Hotham insisted that one be built at Kipling Cotes on the York-Beverley line *(the start of the Kipling Cotes Derby)*. The line does, however, cross the course of this famous race, which is the oldest horse race in Britain (1519), and is run on the third Thursday in March.

The line went into Middleton station, crossing under the bridge of the A163 (which still remains) then continuing towards Bainton, crossing the A163 once again, but over the road this time. The gatehouse can still be seen but now it is a private residence.

25

Bainton station stands approximately a mile south of the village, and can still be seen together with the station workers' houses on the opposite side of the road. The station and out-buildings, together with a large area for vehicle access, are still in splendid condition, used now as a private dwelling. The platform can still be seen, although it has been incorporated into a garden.

The land from Bainton to Southburn levels out as the train approached Driffield, the small minor road leading from Southburn towards Watton crossed the line by bridge, which can still be seen. Parts of where the line ran can also be traced out of the now ploughed-over land, and at Southburn the railway cottages are still to be seen and lived in.

From Southburn where the line crosses the A163 yet again, the gatehouse is once more a private home, over Driffield trout stream and merging with the Malton line across the main Driffield to Beverley road and terminating at Driffield station, before continuing on to the coast.

As well as providing a fast service to the coast from Selby and the West Riding, passengers found they had a shorter route to York, which previously meant changing at Seamer from the Hull-Scarborough train. The opening of the line led to all sorts of possibilities. Direct trains to York were run in the summer months. One major problem on the high Wolds part of the line was the heavy winter snow. In 1950 four engines and a goods train full of sheep were stranded all night whilst workmen worked through the night and most of the following day to free them. The swirling blizzards made it virtually impossible to move the snow fast enough.

For many years Bridlington had an express passenger service to Leeds. It left Bridlington at eight minutes to eight in the morning, stopping only at Driffield and Market Weighton for a York connection, and arrived in Leeds at twenty-four minutes past nine. The return journey left Leeds at eight minutes to five, stopping only at Driffield and arriving back at Bridlington at twenty-two minutes past six. This proved ideal for businessmen living close to the line and working in York or Leeds.

Although in the early days the line was owned by the SB&WRJR, they did not actually have any rolling stock or locomotives, as was the case with many railways of the day, so the line was in fact worked by the NER. This situation continued up to 1913 when the SB&WRJR decided to sell out to NER, because it felt that it was not getting fair treatment from them.

On Monday, October 23rd 1905, the Selby-Market Weighton line played host to its most important train and passenger, the Royal Train conveying King Edward VII and his entourage whilst on a visit to Londesborough Lodge. The train left Kings Cross via Selby and thence on to Market Weighton.

The final demise for the line came with rationalisation under Beeching's axe, when the line was closed down in 1964 to passenger traffic, and to all traffic on June 14th 1965.

B1 4-6-0 (1942), designed by Thompson for LNER

B.16/1 61456 climbs Enthorpe bank with a Leeds-Bridlington train. (1959)

Market Weighton station.

A rare picture taken by A. M. Ross of B1 61010 Wildebeeste leaving the abandoned station at Burdale with a scenic excursion from Hull to Whitby on Bank Holiday Sunday, August 3rd 1958.

CHAPTER FIVE
THE MALTON DODGER (1853-1958)

The Driffield-Malton railway was one half of the service Driffield to Pilmoor and operated in two parts. Another one of George Hudson's schemes and known in its early days as the Malton and Driffield Junction Railway, the line went into operation on May 19th 1853, together with a section that joined the York, Newcastle and Berwick Company line at Pilmoor Junction.

The railway was opened by the usual dignitaries and, on returning to Malton, celebrations were concluded at the "Talbot" where it was left to the Earl of Carlisle to pay a belated and sincere tribute to Hudson for the work, dedication and care that he had personally put into the project. The Earl felt somewhat embarrassed as he delivered the speech, for it was just after the time that George had been caught with his hands in the till, so to speak, and had fallen from grace. Although George was not flavour of the month, his hard work had nevertheless not gone without notice. "I am bound in truth and candour to state that as far as the management of our own line is concerned nothing could exceed the attention and courtesy that we have experienced at the hands of Mr. Hudson," the Earl stated in his concluding words.

In fact Hudson had invested £40,000 of his company's money (YNMR) into the project. This was an excellent move and showed confidence in the venture. It was, however, not looked on favourably by certain members of the board, as he had not obtained a statutory authorisation to do so. This gave his enemies more bullets to fire at a later stage.

Hudson's main purpose for building the line was mainly strategic. He saw it as a guardian to the main approaches of the East Coast. The prosperity for such resorts as Scarborough and Whitby can surely be attributed to Hudson.

The construction of the line had been no easy task; in fact it had proved to present major engineering difficulties. On leaving Driffield the line curved out of the station, crossing the main Driffield to Beverley road, then looping round and heading on to Garton, the station being some mile or so from the village (in many cases they actually served two villages). It then proceeded across the flat plain, crossing the main Driffield to York road, where the old gatehouse can still be seen together with the cutting where the track once lay. Running through a chalk quarry and on to Wetwang, some three miles further along the line, it crossed the Malton to Beverley road, and here again the gatehouse still remains. On crossing this section of the road the train pulled into the Sledmere and Fimber station (now a picnic area). On leaving the station it crossed yet another road before passing Burdale gatehouse, Burdale station and the quarry. It was from then on that the difficulties arose, with the mile-long tunnel through the chalk Wolds and the stubbornness of the rock formation (oolithic limestone) just north of Burdale together with the Peafield cutting and the thousands of tons of stone to provide foundations for the line between Wharram and North Grimston. These difficulties, together with some steep gradients, placed an added, unexpected and heavy burden on the financial side of the line.

From North Grimston the line passed under the road via a small humped-back bridge and on to Settrington station with little difficulty, before making the wide sweep to join the York-Scarborough line and finishing the first leg of its journey at Malton.

King George VI and Queen Elizabeth arriving at Fimber and Sledmere station in 1948, whilst on a visit to Sledmere House.

Fimber gatehouse — Note Mortimer's Mill in the background, public toilets and car park cover the spot.

The line proved its worth in the early days. With both Driffield and Malton being market towns, it was of great benefit to the farmers, a cheap and fast method of getting their stock and goods to market, as well as the villagers being able to travel much more quickly and comfortably.

It was never a busy line with regard to passenger traffic, being a line that was plagued with heavy snow in winter. Nevertheless, it always managed to stay open.

The "Dodger" was withdrawn from service on June 5th 1950, for passengers. Although closed, due to a severe winter that year the line was re-opened to enable food to be transported to the Wold villages. It delivered one thousand pounds of beef and other foodstuffs, which was dropped off at each station along the way for the villages to collect and distribute. The nearest station to the tiny village of Thixendale was Burdale, some four miles away. Villagers had to trudge across the fields in deep snow with sledges; part of the consignment of food left for them were 300 loaves of bread.

As well as providing for the farmers, large amounts of stone were carried from the quarries at Burdale and Wharram.

As stated earlier, the line closed officially to passenger traffic in 1950 (a hundred years after it had been opened) and was only used occasionally to ferry stranded villagers into the town. Eight years later *(20th October 1958)* the freight side was discontinued, and the track lifted.

Although the line is long gone, local people had great affection and fond memories of the *"Dodger,"* regarded as their unfailing friend. This pretty little line, running through some lovely countryside, with its well-kept stations, maintains much evidence still to be seen for the enthusiast. Most of the stations and gatehouses have been turned into private dwellings, but still remain intact. Wharram, North Grimston and Settrington stations still have signs of the platforms, and there are many bridges and a viaduct still to be seen. The ground where the track once lay is in evidence in many places. Possibly the best is where the track ran close to the road prior to pulling into Burdale station.

Many people still remember travelling on the Driffield to Malton line, be it to work, shop or school, and of course the highlight of the line was the occasion when the Royals visited Sledmere House and stayed overnight at Sledmere and Fimber station.

In 1925 King George V and Queen Mary visited the Sledmere Stud as did his son, George VI, and Queen Elizabeth in 1948. Those must have been proud days for the fussy little *"Dodger."*

Workmen closing off Burdale tunnel.

Wetwang looking north, 1956.

32

Fimber and Sledmere station in its heyday.

Garton, 1958.

Raising Steam. Bridlington during the Fifties. *B1 61303* w
bound train. The fine gantry is long gone, and B&Q has taken o
replaced b

eave the shed while tank engine 67640 departs with a Hull
pen space for its superstore, the shed in the background now
r-park.

B.16/1 4-6-0 No. 61469 passes Driffield with the summer Saturday Scarborough-Blackburn, 1956.

Wharram station, early 1900s.

'Twixt' North Grimston and Wharram.

Settrington station.

37

Botanic Gardens station. (Spring Bank)

Withernsea station.
Locomotive being turned ready for the return journey to Hull.

CHAPTER SIX
HULL-WITHERNSEA LINE

As George Hudson's empire crumpled in 1849, so the prominence of Anthony Bannister's rose with his far-sighted vision of linking Hull with Holderness and out on to the east coast, seeing Withernsea as another Brighton, like Hudson's dreams of Whitby and Scarborough.

Bannister was a prominent figure in Victorian Hull and was mainly responsible for the promoting and building of the Hull to Withernsea line, and the servicing of many villages on the way, villages which up to this time had to rely on water transport from Patrington Haven to convey their goods down to Hull and beyond. But as Sunk Island was developing the haven was beginning to silt up. By 1835 the trade in grain had declined so much the possibility of a rail link with Hull offered an enormous market with great potential, serving towns well into the West Riding.

The economics of the line were very favourable. First of all there was no problem in purchasing the land; the landowners were only too willing to oblige. The lay of the land did not present any engineering problems, so a board of directors was set up: Sir Thomas Aston, Clifford Constable of Burton Constable, John George Bowes Thornton Hildyard of Winestead Hall, (Gentleman.) John Crowther Metcalf Harrison, Sheriff of Hull. Henry Cautley of Hedon. (Surgeon.) Arthur Marshall of Headingley, Linen Manufacturer. Thomas Joseph Oust of Keyingham (Gentleman.) Samuel Priestman, East Mount, Sutton. Joseph Walker Pease, Hesslewood House, (Banker.) Christopher Leake Ringrose from Tranby a Merchant. William Marshall MP. Patterdale Hall, Westmorland and the chairman, Anthony Bannister, of High Paull and Lord Mayor of Hull. The treasurer was Arthur Pease of Hull. The line was called "The Hull and Holderness Railway" (H&HR).

Royal assent was granted on July 8th 1853; capital raised was £153,000 through a share issue of 7,500 shares at £20 each and a loan. The line soon got under way; ballast being supplied locally from Kelsey Hill near Burstwick was a great help. Eleven months later in March 1854, the line was completed. Captain Taylor inspected it, and on June 26th 1854 the line was declared open, and the following day to the general public.

Withernsea was not the first choice as the premier resort for the area. A census carried out in 1851 showed only a handful of houses and one shop with 109 people living in the village. The area from Easington up to Tunstall was surveyed and finally Withernsea was decided upon.

The station was built by Cuthbert Broderick and, as it was to be a premier resort for the Victorians to take the water, there had to be a fine hotel. The Station Hotel, later to become known as the Queen's Hotel, was built.

At 11.20am a train left Paragon station for Victoria Dock station, the terminal for the H&HR. As the train approached Hedon the bells rang out from Saint Augustine's Church, with people gathering alongside the line. At Withernsea an imposing crowd had gathered from villages all over the county. Five hundred guests had been invited to the opening ceremony and, whilst they all tucked in to the feast that had been laid on for them, they were oblivious of the strong winds, and slowly the marquee collapsed around them.

39

Anthony Bannister (in Volunteers uniform).

Meanwhile, due to pressing business in Hull, the Lord Mayor, Henry Cooper, arrived on the second train. In the crowd's enthusiasm to toast the new line, all the wine had been drunk so poor old Henry missed out. The celebrations ended promptly at 4.30pm and by 4.50pm the train was on its way back to Hull, arriving at 7pm.

The old ruined church of Saint Nicholas did not give a very attractive picture to the visitor on his arrival at Withernsea, so in true Victorian style they built a pier in 1854. The novelty of the train pulled in 63,764 people within four months, but the line was never really a success, mainly, it is thought, because it was single track, with only one train at a time being allowed.

The H&HR shared the station at Victoria Dock with the Y&NM. However Y&NM ran an unproductive service around the city to Manor House Street and, after withdrawing this service in 1854, the H&HR had the station all to itself. In 1863 they decided it would be better to run trains from Paragon and, in mid-1864, a through service commenced.

The H&HR were a truly independent railway, having their own locos and coaches, unlike many so-called independents who persuaded the NE railway to work their trains, a bit like chartering or contract hire of today.

Sadly on January 1st 1860, the line was leased to the North Eastern line and on July 7th 1862 the Hull and Holderness Railway was dissolved as a company and completely taken over by the NER.

In 1902 the Queen's Hotel with three acres of land was bought by Sir James Reckitt, the industrialist, and presented to the Hull Royal Infirmary to become a convalescent home.

The North Eastern Railway developed the line and introduced a second track to make it a more viable proposition in the early 1900's, but the section between Hedon and Ryehill, and Ottringham and Winestead remained single. Winestead station closed to passenger traffic on July 1st 1904 but remained open to freight up to 1956. Other stations that were closed were Hedon racecourse (all traces gone) and, in 1948, on the old Hedon aerodrome a speedway track was built, with its own halt. It too was closed down. The stations, in an effort to economise, cut back on staff and introduced conductor/guards on diesel railcars. Still losing money, the line was closed on October 19th 1964.

Bannister's dreams for Withernsea of becoming an east coast Brighton were sadly diminished. However Withernsea did grow, possibly not quite to the extent which Bannister had in mind, but today it is a thriving town, with good holiday facilities and caravan parks.

It is fitting that Bannister's name lives on; one of the streets that was actually built to cater for the holiday trade was named after him. Part of the station still remains, although a supermarket stands on the site of the large turntable and an open market at the rear. In the late forties I spent many happy times at Withernsea. I remember how we used to hang out of the carriage windows, trying to be the first to see the lighthouse, and shouting out when we did. To earn pocket money we used to go to the station and wait at the gates with little barrows, taking the holidaymakers' luggage to wherever they were staying. We would get a shilling (5p) or sometimes more. Nothing lasts.

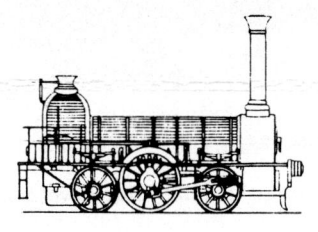

Stepney level crossing. (Beverley Road)

The notorious Anlaby Road level crossing.

42

CHAPTER SEVEN
HULL-HORNSEA LINE (1864-1964)

One of Hudson's schemes was a plan to run a line to Hornsea. It was to branch off at Arram from the Hull-Bridlington line, and terminate somewhere on the Atwick road close to the old mill. Work was to commence in 1847. Unfortunately George's over-ambitious plans came to nothing; he faced ruin due to reckless speculation and shady deals. The line was never built.

It was not until 1862 that work actually started on the Hornsea-Hull line but the route was not that which had been planned by Hudson.

The man behind the project was Mr. Joseph Armytage Wade, a resident of Hornsea and a Hull timber merchant, whose daughter married Samuel Plimsoll, responsible for the prevention of overloading ships (all British merchant ships carry a plimsoll line marked amidships near the water line).

Wade convinced his associates that Hornsea had much more to offer than Withernsea. Hornsea had superior residential amenities, and he wanted to make it a fashionable Victorian watering place.

So the Hull and Hornsea Railway Company was formed in 1861, and in 1862 Lord Hotham introduced the bill before Parliament, the subscribers being Mr. G. A. Wade, Benjamin Haworth, Thomas Sykes, Edward Broosheft, Samuel Egginton and Thomas Haller.

The company had capital of £10,000, and the line was to be completed within five years. On October 8th 1862, a brass band marched from Hornsea House to Bank Terrace in Southgate, watched by local schoolchildren as the turning of the first sod took place by Mr. Wade. He had been presented by the directors with a commemorative spade and an elegant Italian walnut wheelbarrow carved to represent a rhinoceros. Why a rhinoceros? It was part of the Wades' family crest.

The line presented many problems, unlike the Withernsea line. The clay soil proved difficult when it came to building embankments and large amounts of ballast had to be shipped from Kelsey Hill. The line was intended to terminate at Hornsea Bridge and the extension to the final terminus proved very expensive due to piling that had to take place to provide supports for the line where it passed over boggy land.

Labour also proved to be a problem. The "navigators" (navvies) who were responsible for building the canals and railway bridges and tunnels of the day were very well paid, something like £2 10s (£2.50) per week as against a farm labourer's wage of 8/- (40p). After they had got their wages they would go to the nearest pub and stay there till all their money had gone. This could be for as long as five days. Often they were brought before the magistrates and fined for drunkenness. This led to delays; in fact the line was two months overdue on the completion date.

Wade must have had a good teacher in Hudson, for one of Hudson's favourite fiddles was to buy land cheaply and then sell it to his own company at an inflated price. Wade too was accused of doing this; the whole affair was instigated by Bannister (Hull-Withernsea line).

On completion in 1864, Captain Rich, the Government inspector, had difficulties when he came to inspect the line, for the line had gone to the west of Stoneferry road instead of east as specified in the original act. He was not satisfied with the work that had been carried out at Marton and other

43

Austerity 2-8-0 built for wartime service in 1942.
Designed by R. A. Riddles.

crossings, remarking that they were below standard. Whilst examining a bridge he fell into Sutton Drain. This was not guaranteed to help things along as the builders and officials could not contain their amusement.

Difficulties plus the delays caused serious financial losses to Wade. In October 1863, Mr. R. G. Wade, the eldest son of Mr. J. A. Wade, laid the foundation stone for Hornsea station and the line opened to traffic on Easter Monday, March 28th 1864.

The estimate for building the line had been £68,000; the actual cost at the end of the day was £122,000.

The line started at Wilmington station; arrangements with the North Eastern Railway were not complete to run from Paragon until June 1st 1864. The first train with sixteen carriages was filled with passengers, despite the miserable weather. A band played inside one of the carriages, and people lined the station to witness the departure at noon. All went well and the first train into Hornsea arrived at one o'clock to be greeting by the firing of a cannon and a procession. Teas were served, all at the personal expense of Wade. He tried to impress on the people of Hornsea how important the line was in developing the town, but Hornsea people were slow to respond, possibly one of the early nails in the railway's coffin. Hornsea people were not over keen at wanting, let alone encouraging, visitors to the town, and certainly not day trippers.

The line in all its existence never witnessed an accident. At first it was run on a single track using rolling stock provided by North Eastern Railways, but after only two years the NER took them over because of financial problems, and in 1900 a double track was laid.

In 1910-12 Wilmington was rearranged and was built above ground level to dispense with the level crossing; and a new swing bridge over the River Hull was built. The old station named Sculcoates was closed and the new station called Wilmington was opened. Half a mile out of the station the line curved in an easterly direction, parting company with the Withernsea line and heading for the coast, the first station being Sutton, before turning in a northerly direction to Swine and Skirlaugh. Ellerby station was closed in 1902 and twenty years later Burton Constable was renamed Ellerby to prevent confusion with another line. Hatfield station for some obscure reason was called Sigglesthorne, which was a good three miles away, the line then finally passing through Goxhill before Hornsea Bridge and Hornsea Town.

1960 saw the same economic measures as were taken with the Withernsea line, but these failed to save the inevitable closure of the Hull and Hornsea Railway on October 19th 1964.

CHAPTER EIGHT
HULL AND BARNSLEY LINE (1885-1964)

The Hull and Barnsley Railway was one of the last complete and independent Victorian railways to be built, and built at very great cost. Probably the most ambitious track ever laid in East Yorkshire opened in July 1885; not, I might add, a line built through railway mania as was the reason in many cases, but with the sole intention of breaking the monopoly of the North Eastern Railway, who controlled all the freight. At that time Hull was the only town of its size to be served by just one railway company.

The coming of the H&B eased the congestion and total chaos that had occurred on the docks, which had held Hull back as a port. With a new dock the city prospered.

A new company was formed in 1879. Ironically the meeting was held at The Royal Station Hotel, North Eastern territory. Land was purchased and a new dock was built in Hull with first-class coal handling facilities, and a direct rail link with the coal fields of South Yorkshire and the West Riding.

Hull had always been starved of good steam coal because of the North Eastern's policy of carrying the softer West Yorkshire coal at 2/7d (13p) per ton and the South Yorkshire coal at 3/1d (15p) per ton. This higher rate made it difficult for the port to compete with its rival, the Manchester Sheffield and Lincolnshire Railway, which carried cheap coal to Grimsby.

The H&B line went literally straight through the Wolds. The choice of route was based on earlier surveys and, because the NER occupied both the Humber Bank and the gap in the Wolds at Market Weighton, there was little choice. So, with a compromise reached, the line climbed the Wolds to a height of 250 feet. Its contruction had involved channelling and tunnelling through the Wold's chalk and cutting started west of Great Gutter Lane, Willerby. The earth dug out formed the long embankment down to Springhead. The heaviest excavation work was at "Big Hill" or Little Weighton cutting. The rock was used on the embankments on the western approaches to Hull.

The cost of the whole project was a massive six million pounds. In fact the line was in financial difficulties before it even opened. There were recommendations to abandon the grandiose station to be built in Kingston Square, where the New Theatre stands today. With further solutions being put forward, the extra funds were finally raised and the Alexandra Dock opened on July 16th 1885. The line opened for goods traffic on July 20th and for passenger traffic one week later.

On leaving Alexandra Dock the line ran around the northern part of the city on an embankment, and crossed the main roads by bridges instead of the dreaded level crossings, that were to prove a nightmare in later years, bestowed on the city by the North Eastern. There were 35 bridges within the city boundary. The bridge at Beverley Road was unique; the 1880 Act stressed that it had to be of an ornamental design to be approved by the Corporation but the decoration was destroyed in the last war. The bridge over Newland Toft Lane (Newland Avenue) was also of a decorative kind.

Cannon Street station was originally intended for carriage sheds and goods yard, with the passenger station close to the city centre as mentioned earlier. The situation of Cannon Street was inconvenient and in poor surroundings, the buildings unpretentious and accommodation for passengers very small, with coal yards on both sides of the passengers'

45

W.D. 2-8-0. No. 90322 passes over South Cave with coal for Hull.

Mathew Stirling's express passenger loco 4-4-0s built in 1910 for the Hull and Barnsley Railway.

Drewton Dale and tunnel (1932).

approach. This did nothing to enhance the image of the company. On leaving the station the line was lifted to embankment level and curved to join the main line from the docks at Beverley Road junction where there was a more popular station with greater accessibility and a tram service to the city centre.

After passing Springhead Works and out of Hull, the first station was Willerby and Kirkella, situated between the two villages. The line then climbed to its summit at Little Weighton, passing over the famous Eppleworth viaduct, and then fell at a rate of 1/150 through Drewton Tunnel, which was some 2,116 yards long, before the line emerged into Weedley Dale and then on to South Cave Station, which was on the northern edge of the village. The line then proceeded on to North Cave, Newport, Sandholme, North Eastrington, South Howden and on into the West Riding.

A determined effort was made to build up the passenger side of the business, the first passenger train leaving Cannon Street on July 27th 1885. The inconvenience of the stations was blamed for the small numbers of people travelling. The journey from Hull to Cudworth in 1885 took 88 minutes and a third class fare 4/4¼ (22p), second class 6/- (30p), first class 7/6 (37¼p). In 1896 there was the introduction of a night mail, and in 1902 football excursions were developed successfully to the West Riding. These lasted up to the First World War. Excursions to Little Weighton and South Cave were introduced in 1904 to run on a Sunday for 6d (2½p) with much disgust and many complaints. One such person, John Waudby of South Cave, made such statements as "the undesirables of Hull bringing with them a stream of immorality." The company replied "it was desirable to enable hard-working men to enjoy a time in the country."

Another excursion from Hull to Leeds was the Cookes excursion. This left Hull every Saturday at 1pm returning from Leeds at 10.45pm (one hour later during the pantomime season). The fare was 2/- (10p).

47

Bridlington shed, 53D, some time in the late fifties. Lined up awaiting their turn for duty are two K3s, a D49 and a Black Five. All the area shown is now covered by B&Q's car park.

This picture brings back happy memories for the photographer. It won 2s. 6d. in a photographic competition in Meccano Magazine. 4-4-0 62667 "Somme" awaits departure at Bridlington's platform seven, some time in the early fifties.

48

It is interesting to note that ninety-five per cent of all immigrants passing through England from Europe to North America were handled in Hull. The H&B made provision for this traffic and they provided accommodation for them on Alexandra Dock. The boats docked Fridays or Saturdays and the immigrants often camped in Pearsons Park whilst waiting for the trains to leave on Mondays from Cannon Street.

The building of the line took a considerable work force and the H&B employed over 8,000 navvies aged from 10 to 70 years. They came from all over Britain, a large number were Scottish and Irish and there was continual fighting between these two factions. The navvies lived mostly in camps; the largest of these was at Riplingham on top of the tunnel. Other camps in the area were at Hull Bridge, Springhead and Wyke Street. Some of them lived in small huts dotted along the line. The Riplingham camp had its own shops and mission church and the navvies' children attended the local village school at Little Weighton.

Riots broke out frequently between Irish and English navvies, at Riplingham and Springhead in 1882 the company sacked 200 of each nationality. Most of these men worked from dawn until dusk six days a week, the average wage for a 58-hour week was 30/- (£1.50). In May 1881, 700 men went on strike for an extra 6d (2¼d) per week. On the whole, labour relations were considered to be good. The company's financial difficulties also affected the navvies; when work stopped for five months in July 1884 all the navvies become unemployed and the majority of them stayed on.

The North Eastern Railway, faced with competition, began to reduce their charges, but up to the First World War the H&B had made handsome profits for its shareholders. Now it was faced with stiffer competition.

1923 brought the grouping together of small companies into four major conglomerates. However the H&B had already been swallowed up a year earlier by the North Eastern after thirty-seven years as an independent railway.

The writing was on the wall. Many of the employees at the Springhead Works were transferred to Darlington, locomotives, buildings and everything that went into portraying the individuality of an independent railway were maintained for a time, some modified and some sold off.

Cannon Street, the main passenger terminal, was closed down in 1924 and subsequently demolished, although it is still possible to locate the site. For a time trains appeared on the north side of Paragon Station. Parts of the line ceased in 1932. A service of sorts ran as far as South Howden up to August 1955 when that too faded away. There was a few years of brisk trade from the collieries of South Yorkshire bringing coal one way and taking pit props on the return journey. In 1964 the main line closed, leaving the elevated section round the city from the docks to a new connection at the Hessle Road junction.

Springhead works finally closed in 1972 and a short section of the track near Drax Power Station is all that remains.

Many of the stations have disappeared but there are still remains of the South Cave station in our area, sadly not as grand looking as it was in its days of glory. The country stations on the H&B were fine buildings.

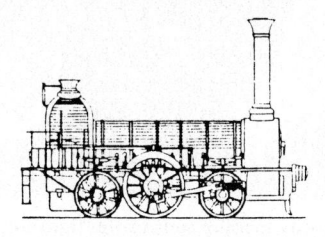

49

LNER Y8 No. 559 leaving Patrington for Kilnsea in 1940 on loan to Spurn Railway.

"Kenyan," 2-4-0 saddle tanker.

Spurn Railway looking south from lighthouse

CHAPTER NINE
A LITTLE RAILWAY AT SPURN

The building of a railway at Spurn Point goes back to approximately 1912 just prior to the First World War. The reasons for a line to be built on such a remote part of the East Yorkshire coast was mainly out of necessity.

Spurn had always been a vulnerable spot for an invasion from across the North Sea throughout its long history. Most of Britain's invaders of the past had viewed Spurn as an easy, unprotected landing place. In fact it was considered a vital part of our sea defences in guarding the major port of Hull. The War Department purchased the peninsula from the Constable family.

The line itself was built to transport materials for defence work, and to build a sea wall some 300 yards long on the seaward side of Kilnsea village. The main defence works at Kilnsea were known as the Goodwin Battery, and Spurn, the Green Battery, plus the two forts out in the Humber estuary Bull Sand Fort and Haile Sands Fort off Cleethorpes.

Getting the materials to such an out-of-the-way place posed major problems. There was already a train service in operation from Hull to Withernsea, with the nearest station to Kilnsea at Patrington. The problem arose over the distance between Patrington and Kilnsea. The roads were very bad, uneven, narrow and twisting, and in many places little more than dirt tracks, with no road at all between Kilnsea and Spurn. To transport machinery and materials over such roads would have been hazardous to say the least. It was decided to bring the materials required down river by barge to a jetty on the river side at the end of the peninsula, and run a railway line up to Kilnsea.

A railway line in preference to a road was much cheaper and easier to lay, and could be taken up at a moment's notice at little cost or trouble should the occasion arise. Also rolling stock was easily available with many contractors already having it in their possession.

Contracts to carry out the work were awarded to J. C. Willis of Manchester and London who had been involved in railway and dock construction in earlier years.

The line was secondhand stock bought from the Manchester-Sheffield and Lincolnshire Railway Company, and the first locomotive was "Somerton," built by Hudswell Clarke to haul contractors' paddy wagons on the GWR's Tyseley and Stratford on Avon line. The second locomotive was "Bombay," which had spent most of its life working on the docks at Dagenham; also "Kenyon" built in 1888 and "Frances" and "Lord Mayor," all saddle tank engines. The length of the line makes its probably one of the shortest in the country, discounting mine railways, a total of three and a quarter miles of single track with passing loops.

The jetty was 270 feet long and 18 feet wide and built fifty yards beyond the lifeboat slipway and was tee-shaped. The line went to the end of the jetty. At the Kilnsea end of the line were the officers' mess, hospital and barracks, a rocket post and the Blue Bell Inn. The line stayed after the contractors had left and was officially taken over by the War Department in 1918.

During the war there were five steam locomotives in use and an hourly service between 9.30am to 4pm; also on the line was a wind bogie and a converted "Itala" racing car.

51

Lifeboatmen using sail bogie

The wind bogie was used mainly by the lifeboatmen when the steam trains weren't running to get up to the pub at Kilnsea. If the wind was strong it could blow them over; in fact a top speed of 40mph was recorded, and if there was no wind they ended up pushing it. One of the main problems was drifting sand — it would entirely cover the line.

In 1918 Lieutenant Lees of the Royal Engineers had his men convert a motor car to run on the line for his own personal use, a sporting pre-1914 vintage model two-seater.

On January 21st 1920, the first official railcar was despatched to the Spurn Head Garrison. It was a Drewery petrol railcar and it came by rail to Patrington and then by road to Kilnsea. The "Hardy," a much larger railcar built at Slough, soon followed, and was in use up to the end of World War Two. HRH Princess Royal visited the peninsula and travelled on the line.

From 1924 to 1927 an enterprising char-a-banc owner advertised in the local Hull paper: "Excursions to Kilnsea with a train ride to Spurn Point." This was all quite unofficial, and ceased as soon as the "Top Brass" found out about it. In 1936 the Lord Mayor of Hull arranged holidays for children with accommodation in the army buildings. The highlight of the holiday was a trip on the railway to Spurn.

For fourteen years prior to the line closing, most of the driving was done by Mr. Van Leagh, a civilian employee who lived at Keyingham. During the war he would start his day at 7am taking Service personnel going on leave from Spurn up to Kilnsea to join the bus for Hull.

World War Two increased traffic on the line and extra rolling stock was transferred from the LNER, but in 1951 all the rolling stock was sold off and the line taken up and bought by Thomas W. Ward Ltd.

Hudswell Clarke P.265 on the Spurn Head Railway

Mr. W. C. Harding and wife with passengers on sail bogie

The opening of the line at Wheldrake station.

DVLR railcars

54

CHAPTER TEN
THE DERWENT VALLEY LIGHT RAILWAY
(1913-1982)

On March 21st 1898, the Riccall District Council met to make a decision on a railway and the proposal was carried unanimously. The railway was the Derwent Valley Light Railway. It was suggested that it would run from Cliff Common through Skipwith, North Duffield, Thorganby, West Cottingwith, Wheldrake, Sutton, Newton, Kexby, Dunnington and terminate at Stamford Bridge. There was, however, dissatisfaction shown at this proposed route.

A line from Knottingley via Selby through Riccall and Escrick and then on to Bridlington and Scarborough was more favourable and would make them more independent of the NER. However, this proposition was not considered practical.

A further meeting was held on May 29th 1899, when it was decided that the line would commence at Foss Island in York and terminate at Cliff Common on the NER's Selby-Market Weighton line, for which no problems were foreseen.

The line was authorised on September 29th 1899, and was to be called "The Derwent Valley Light Railway." It was in 1895 within the Queen's Speech that new legislation was brought out which, it was hoped, would be beneficial to rural communities.

Farming was in the doldrums. The Light Railways Act of 1896 was created in an effort to help farmers get their produce to markets at low cost. So, after much discussion and argument, on August 14th 1896, the Light Railways Act became law.

In effect the Act replaced the expensive and cumbersome procedure which had scuttled so many schemes in the past, with public inquiries into where the lines would run by the Railways Commission, who would then pass it over to the Board of Trade. Engineers' and legal fees had to be met and the whole procedure for a small railway like the DVLR was expensive and not a viable proposition. The Light Railways Act did away with all that.

What constitutes a "light railway"? The term is an elusive one, as there are no precise guidelines laid down. They need not be of a smaller gauge than four feet eight and a half inches, although many of them are narrower, and they usually have only a single track, together with sharper curves and steeper gradients. This reduces the amount of work in laying the track. The locos and rolling stock are usually lighter in axle weight, and speed is usually restricted to 25mph.

There were many advantages to be derived from the Light Railways Act; signals were not required, stations were but platforms and shelters were not mandatory, continuous brakes were not essential because of the low speeds. Also fencing could be dispensed with, level crossing gates were not required so long as cattle guards were provided, and speed reduced when nearing the crossings (although some were added later).

On November 27th 1906, objections were heard by the Board of Trade, the objectors being the parish councils of Cliff, Osgodby, South Duffield and Kellfield (because there would be no benefits derived from the railway), together with 260 landowners and many ratepayers. Faced with such opposition, the Board of Trade adjourned their decision. However the Order was granted in 1907, and the capital of the company was fixed at £81,000 in one pound shares.

55

Thorganby station

Both the Riccall and Escrick Rural District Councils were obliged to advance an annual sum without interest, £600 and £900 respectively, repayment to be secured by sinking fund policies.

Building the line did not present any problems, the land being level except for the odd cutting, largest being about thirty feet at Dunnington. This was of great interest as they dug out ice-polished boulders of immense size, and at Skipwith Common, of great interest to geologists, was the famous "gullery."

The northern end of the line was situated in Hallfield Road, York, joining the Foss Island branch of British Railways. The station was to be called Layerthorpe. There was a large yard and exchange sidings, together with warehouses, and a single long platform, engine shed and general offices. All the lines converged into a single track east of the station, proceeding to Osbaldwick, Murton Lane and Dunnington Halt before turning south and following the course of the River Derwent, which too had been a busy thoroughfare in its time, transporting coal, oil-cake, grain, malt, etc. These were carried by barge to Stamford Bridge and Malton prior to the construction of the railway.

From Elvington, which also served the village at the other side of the river, Sutton on Derwent, the line made its way down to Wheldrake, Cottingwith, Thorganby, Skipwith and North Duffield, terminating with NER's Selby-Market Weighton branch line at Cliff Common.

The total distance from Layerthorpe to Cliff was sixteen miles and one chain of standard gauge single track, which was obtained from the old Midland Railway of the Settle-Carlisle line. The steepest gradient of 1 in 150 for three-quarters of a mile was between Dunnington and Murton, and throughout the whole length there were only two over bridges. When a new housing estate at Melrosegate in York was built a further overhead bridge had to be constructed over the line.

At each station the buildings had their own unique style, built on brick foundations, with wood plaster panels. There were offices and waiting rooms together with a public convenience, with ample sidings and high loading docks and goods sheds at main stations.

The cost of constucting the DVLR was £7,852 per mile, which also included the price of the land. There were no signals, with the exception of one at Wheldrake to take into account a sharp curve, which obscured the view of the level crossing. The mechanism for the signal could not have been simpler: it was connected by a pulley to the nearside gate with a counter-weight to maintain the tension on the rope. This simple Heath Robinson contraption was designed and made in a joiner's workshop on the Sand Hutton estate.

Late in December 1912, there was still over four miles of track to lay, due mainly to lack of funds and the contractors being unable to meet their debts, with a cat-and-mouse game being played out by contractors and bailiffs in an effort to impound the locomotive.

Finally, on July 19th 1913, the day had arrived for the opening of the line, and the question of a ceremony to mark this auspicious occasion arose. It was decided that a trial run should take place, with a luncheon funded by the directors afterwards.

Invitations were sent out to the Chairman and Clerks of the two District Councils, The Lord Mayor, Sheriff, and Town Clerks of the City of York, Mr. Butcher, KC, MP, Mr. Rowntree, MP, Mr. Harrison-Broadley, MP, Mr. F. H. Anderson, six NER officials, the Engineer, his assistant, and three of the contractor's staff.

The opening ceremony was to be performed by Lady Deramore, who was the wife of the chairman of the line. The engine was connected by blue silk ribbon to the station at Layerthorpe. Lady Deramore cut the engine free. the guard then blew his whistle and engine NER number 1679, all decked out for

Layerthorpe station, York.

Skipwith station

the occasion, steamed out of York (The DVLR did not have any rolling stock or engine of its own so the NER provided them. The carriages were painted in deep blue with gold lettering) to the shouts and cheers of the crowds that had gathered, pulling two coaches and two decorated open goods wagons with awnings fitted. (No doubt there would have been a band.).

As the train slowed down to go through each station, crowds of cheering people, bubbling with excitement, thronged the platforms, with many young children waving flags.

The official service went into operation on Monday, July 21st 1913, with three classes of travel: 1st Class 3d per mile, 2nd Class 2d per mile and 3rd Class 1p per mile.

During the war years 1914-18 the line was scheduled as an alternative route from York to Selby should the NER line be at any time disrupted.

Like most railways the DVLR suffered from competition as the roads improved. They had to made drastic reductions in their rates and think of other ways to encourage people on to the line. One such idea was a tourist attraction advertising the charming villages on the route and the natural beauties of the Vale of Derwent to the holidaymaker, anglers, walkers, picnic parties and nature lovers, together with comfortable accommodation, good food and moderate charges.

There was also the "Blackberry Specials," when passengers, alighting at Skipwith, would split up into parties, carrying buckets, bags and baskets, and be directed by the Station Master's wife to the best areas. Some six hours later they would return to the station with every type of container full to the brim (Who said "pick your own" was an invention of the 80's?). To help boost trade a free bus service was provided from the villages of Sutton and Elvington to the station by Mr. A. Dawson of the Grey Horse Inn, Elvington. The one proviso was that a return ticket to York or Cliff Common was purchased totalling a shilling from the carrying agent.

On market days during the First World War the DVLR worked trains into Selby over the NER line with a special brake van being inscribed "For use between Selby and Cliff Common."

At its peak 49,983 people travelled on the line 1915, with a revenue of £1,153. In an effort to increase revenue the company dispensed with the third class and re-painted its carriages to second class. This did not prove to be a popular move. By the end of the war road transport was on the increase, and the railway gave way to the roads.

In 1925 things were looking black for the line, with only 18,430 people using it, and receipts down to £664. A decision to close the line to passenger traffic was taken a year later, with the exception of special excursions being run. One such excursion for farmers in the region was to the Royal Show at Harrogate in 1929, run in conjunction with the LNER through Layerthorpe, then by reserved coach to the main line York station.

The goods side of the business was made up of livestock traffic, potatoes, grain, hay and straw, oil-cake, manure, roadstone and timber, but this too went into decline for much the same reason as the passenger traffic had.

Due also to the decline of horse-drawn traffic in Leeds and Hull in the late twenties, and the increased use of chemical fertilisers, stable manure was used less and less by the farmers in the Derwent Valley area. An interesting point was that in an effort to increase crop yield, the company purchased from Northern Command at Catterick Camp the whole output of horse manure from three cavalry units at a cost of one shilling a ton. It was loaded on to the line at the camp's station and carried at a low rate to Layerthorpe by LNER. When the camp became mechanised this trade too was lost, although it had proved to be a very successful move, with never any trouble in getting the farmers to purchase the manure all the year round.

Another sales gimmick was to supply all the farmers in the area with a free newspaper, "The Derwent Farmers' News." It was printed and posted free to all farmers, paid for by advertisers.

Cliffe Common station

Thorganby station.

In 1929, with a prolific potato crop, in an effort to help out farmers the DVLR offered to carry them at a fifty percent reduction in rates. This was much appreciated by the farmers and merchants.

In 1952 Wheldrake was chosen to store thousands of tons of sugar, corned beef, flour and biscuits. The Ministry of Works purchased land in Wheldrake station yard and built a large warehouse as a "buffer depot." The goods were received and sent by rail.

Most of the rolling stock of the DVLR was provided by the NER, but over the years the company accumulated waggons and coaches of their own. In 1925 they purchased a 100hp "Sentinel" *shunting engine No.6076*, it was the first of its kind ever to be tried out on a British railway. It was built at Shrewsbury and the DVLR's big brothers LMS and LNER waived all charges for the loco being delivered over their lines. In a reciprocating gesture the company loaned the loco to LNER for a trial period so that they could assess its value and, although pleased with its performance, it was not suitable for the amount of traffic they handled.

The loco made a considerable saving to the company, but due to the continuing increase in road traffic the DVLR decided to develop Layerthorpe as a coal distribution centre. This proved very successful but the "Sentinel" could not cope with the increase in traffic. She was put up for sale, and sold to a firm in Darlington.

In the late thirties many railways were brought under government control. The DVLR was not one of them. With the imminent outbreak of war the company was worried that, should certain rail heads be closed down, this would have an adverse effect on the line. An effort was made to get the government to take them over, with little success. Sites on the railway were then offered to various government departments, without much interest.

The line became neglected and covered in weeds. This was what saved the line from closure. The RAF took aerial photographs of the line from a height of 3,000 feet. There was nothing to be seen; it was completely camouflaged. Orders were given that no one should touch the line, and stations on the line were used as dumps for the collection of scrap metal.

In 1942 an ordnance supply depot was opened at Layerthorpe by the WD for the storage of Ford engines and spares. These were sent by rail in large quantities.

Murton Lane station was also requisitioned by the WD. This was the Northern Command petrol depot. It was stored in four gallon cans in yards and fields. Over 500,000 gallons were stored. Special trains worked this traffic, being loaded by the troops billeted there.

In 1941 the railway helped in the construction of Elvington aerodrome, carrying thousands of tons of steel and cement. Once operative the cargo changed to bombs. Elvington was manned by the Free French Air Force as a bombing station. It was taken over in 1952 by the WD and used for storage of ammunition which arrived by rail.

Wheldrake station was used as a base for motor spirit which then went on to Melbourne aerodrome. Its main use was to burn off the fog on the runways by fine sprays of fuel being ignited, known as "Operation Fido."

Melbourne alone burnt 1,921,628 gallons in less than two years. One incident occurred when an extra train-load of fuel arrived with nowhere to store it. It was lit up to get rid of it, on a perfectly clear sunny day.

Cottingwith station was requisitioned by the WD for the storage of mustard gas and incendiary bombs. This was a top secret base, but everyone in the village knew about it before it was even taken over.

The mustard gas was pumped into large underground containers, lined with lead, each holding 200 tons. It was never used, but stayed there until 1954, when it was dispatched for disposal at sea.

Layerthorpe at a later date became a depot for aviation fuel, used by planes at Lynton and Full Sutton.

204 hp Loco entering Dunnington Station passing over the A1079 York— Hull road.

There were no major incidents on the line except for a couple of incendiary bombs dropping at Tang Hall on September 24th 1942. There was little damage or inconvenience.

Beeching's axe could not fall on the DVLR. Nevertheless, it was affected by the closure of the Selby-Market Weighton line. This resulted in the company applying for an abandonment order to terminate the Cliff to Wheldrake section of the line, which was granted on February 9th 1965. From then on it was downhill for the DVLR. However, enthusiasts kept the line alive for many years and for a short period of time it ran as far as Dunnington with special excursions from Layerthorpe, finally closing down in 1982.

Although the railway had initially been built to serve the needs of the agricultural community, many small and large commercial developments appeared along it in the shape of storage and depots for further distribution: Russian Oil Products used Murton Lane, Dunnington had a wood yard and grain drying plant, Elvington station carried out waggon repairs, Wheldrake and Skipwith stored fertilisers in nissen huts, Layerthorpe stored coal, and Osbaldwick had a concrete mixing plant, so the line did much in the way of bringing business and work into the area.

The weekly wage of the Station Masters in 1912 when the line opened was 25 shillings per week (£1.25) whilst porters and plate-layers received 15/- (75p), and that was for working over twelve hours a day, starting at 6.30am through to 7pm.

Layerthorpe through to Cliff Common shows little sign of the DVLR. Being built upon for another generation and another need, there are still signs of the line if you look carefully. North Duffield and Wheldrake stations are still intact; bridges and cuttings still remain.

Chapter Eleven
North Holderness Light Railway

The story of the North Holderness Light Railway or, as it was also known, Beverley and Beeford Light Railway, began way back in 1897. Notice was given to construct a light railway from Beverley to a point between North Frodingham and Beeford.

The main subscribers were Henry Llewellen Chowen, Andrew Cochrane, James Jonathon Harrison, Joseph Hannath and William Henry Preston. Capital raised was £40,000 in 8000 £5.00 shares.

The railway was to be divided up into four sections. and commence in a field to the east side of Beverley Station in the parish of St. Martin. Two acres of land was to be set aside for a Passenger Station and Goods Depot together with Sidings and Engine Sheds, turn-table and other necessary buildings.

The line was then to proceed in a north-easterly direction across Cherry Tree Lane entering the Parish of St. Nicholas 18 yards to the north of Mr. Frederick Marsden's cottage. Crossing Swinemoor Lane 30 yards to the south of a row of cottages known as William's Parade, it went in a south-easterly direction to the south-east corner of a grass field on the north side of Grovehill Road which was occupied by the Tigar's Manure Company close to Barmston Drain. At this point an acre of land was to be set aside for the construction of a passenger station and goods depot.

Crossing Barmston Drain on the north side of the present bridge, it skirted the south side of the triangular piece of ground adjoining the River Hull occupied by Messrs Cochrane and Cooper. A multi-purpose swing bridge was to be constructed to take the line over the river and into the parish of Weel.

After crossing the river the line was to turn in a northerly direction, passing the north-west corner of Hoggard House at a distance of about 60 yards, and the north-west corner of New Holland House at a distance of about 70 yards, terminating at a lane in Ticton Carrs 520 yards to the south side of the Beverley/Bridlington road. An acre of land was to be set aside here for the construction of a Passenger Station and Goods Depot.

This section was to end the part of the railway known as Railway Number One, the length being 2½ miles at a cost of £8,875.14s.0d.

Railway Two was to commence in the parish of Ticton by a junction with Railway One, proceeding in an easterly direction, crossing Meaux-Lane at a point 200 yards south of the north-east corner of the Manor House in the parish of Routh. One acre of land was to be set aside for a Passenger Station and Goods Depot. The line was to proceed in a north-easterly direction across the Whitecross-road at North Carr Bridge, with provision for a Passenger Station and Goods Depot. The line would then veer in a northerly direction, crossing the drain adjoining Leven Grange, in the parish of Leven, 470 yards east of the road from Beverley, terminating in a field on the north side of the Hornsea road, at a point about 50 yards east of the junction of High-stile with East Street.

One and a quarter acres of land was to be set aside for the purpose of a Parcel Depot and Passenger Station.

The length of this section of line was five miles. The cost of Railway Number Two was £2,429 3s. 10d.

Railway Number Three was to commence in the parish of Leven by a junction with Railway Number Two and to continue northerly, crossing Loughland Road 300 yards east of the junction of that road with the road from Leven to Brandesburton, then crossing the same road at a point 490 yards north-east of Starcarr-gate, passing the south-east corner of the occupation road in front of the blacksmith's shop in the parish of Brandesburton, occupied by George Bassingdale. The line to continue across Charter Lane and the lane leading from Mill Lane to the Brandesburton and Beeford Road, terminating on the east side of the Brandesburton to Frodingham Road, in a garden occupied by George Eastwood, where one acre of land would be required for Passenger Station and Goods Depot.

The length of Railway Number Three was 1½ miles, at a cost of £2,902 12s. 6d.

Railway Number Four would commence in the Parish of Brandesburton by a junction with Railway Number Three and proceed in a north-easterly direction for a distance of thirty chains, before continuing in a northerly direction, passing the east side of the farm-house known as Mooredge Farm, at a distance of 150 yards, then across the occupation road called Green Lane where half an acre of land would be required for the purpose of sidings.

The line would then continue still northerly through the parishes of Moor Town and North Frodingham, crossing Grange Road 30 yards from the east side of Mr. William Wood's cottage and on to the boundary of the parishes of North Frodingham and Beeford, then turning to a north-westerly direction alongside the east side of the boundary for a distance of half a mile before turning once more to a northerly direction to the south side of Inholm-lane in the parish of North Frodingham, at a point 45 yards west of Inholm Bridge.

At this point the line would terminate, and two acres of land would be purchased for Passenger Station, Goods Depot, sidings, engine sheds and turntable and any other buildings that might be required.

The length of Railway Number Four was 3¾ miles and the cost for this section £7,011 8s. 6d. The total length of the railway from Beverley to Beeford was 12¾ miles. In addition to the land purchased for stations and sidings etc, a further 35 acres was required for the permanant way and other purposes of the railway.

Plans of the proposed work were drawn up and put on public display at the office of Arthur Mills, Solicitors, 62, Whitefriarsgate, in the City of Hull. Copies of the draft order could be obtained on the payment of one shilling, and all objections to the proposals had to be made in writing to the Commissioners on a sheet of foolscap paper, written on one side only, and addressed to The Light Railways Commission, 23, George Street, London, SW. Dated 22nd, April 1897.

The multi-purpose swing bridge to be built at Grovehill was designed to enable it to take foot passengers, carts and cattle for which tolls were to be charged. Foot passengers ½d. Two wheeled vehicles and one horse 2d. Four wheeled cart and horse 4d. Horses, mules, donkeys and cattle 1d per head. Sheep, pigs, goats and lambs 4d per score. Cycles, handcarts and wheelbarrows 1d.

Fares to be charged for rail travel were: First Class 3d per mile, Second Class 2d per mile, Third Class 1d per mile with a minimum charge of 3 miles.

So that is the story of the North Holderness Light Railway. After all the surveying work and the drawing up of plans, the railway was never built. Was it because of the marsh lands; had the surveyors considered it a non-starter? Was the cost at the end of the day too much?

It was even considered to reduce the gauge to 2 feet 8 inches, making it a narrow gauge railway. I have been informed from a reliable source *(the son of the Station Master at the time, Frederick Cooper)* that plans for engines and rolling stock for a narrow gauge railway were drawn up. This would fit in with the theory of the land being too wet; a lighter track and rolling stock would make more sense.

Another possible reason could have been the arrival of the motor bus. North Eastern Railways introduced a bus onto the route in October 1903, retaining the parcel offices that the North Holderness Light Railway had set up prior to the line being built. Therefore, it would have been sound business sense to forget about the railway. The hey days of the railways was on the decline, with a new era commencing, that of the motor coach and providing a bus service was a much cheaper option.

In 1920 Louis J. Stuart formed a company called the Newington Motor and Engineering Company, operating from a garage at 53 Walton Street in Hull. Stuart bought a Maudslay charabanc to do private hire work, and a few months later applied for, and was granted a licence to operate a service from Hull to Beverley, opening a depot at Beverley.

Continuing his expansion he acquired J. Pocklington's licence to operate a service to Hornsea, giving him the chance to run a circular route from Beverley, Brandesburton, Hornsea and Ellerby. He purchased more vehicles and extended his service from Brandesburton to Beeford and then onto Bridlington.

The Newington Company were operating in direct competition with North Eastern Railways who had been operating a bus service from Beverley to Beeford along the route of what was to have been the Holderness Light Railway. North Eastern sold out to Stuart in 1923. Louis Stuart died in 1926 with his son Arthur taking over the business, but he sold out to Hull City Motor Works, later to be absorbed by Kingston Motors in 1929.

A light railway had also been planned to run from Bridlington to Beeford via Carnaby this too never got beyond the planning stage, was this another victim of the bus?

North Eastern Railways Coach, Registration BT 44
The first coach to run between Brandesburton and Beverley.

NORTH EASTERN RAILWAY

MOTOR BUS TIMETABLE

		a.m	a.m	p.m	p.m
BEVERLEY STN. YARD	dep	8.30	10.15	2.0	5.20
HULL BRIDGE	"	8.43	10.28	2.13	5.33
TICKTON	"	8.50	10.35	2.20	5.40
ROUTH	"	9.1	10.46	2.31	5.51
WHITE CROSS	"	9.12	10.57	2.42	6.2
LEVEN	"	9.22	11.7	2.52	6.12
BRANDESBURTON	"	9.37	11.22	3.7	6.27
NORTH FRODINGHAM	"	10.5	11.50	3.35	6.55
BEEFORD	arr	10.20	12.5	3.50	7.10
		a.m	a.m	p.m	p.m
BEEFORD	dep	7.35	11.15	1.30	5.0
NORTH FRODINGHAM	"	8.10	11.30	1.45	5.15
BRANDESBURTON	"	8.38	11.58	2.13	5.43
LEVEN	"	8.53	12.13	2.28	5.58
WHITE CROSS	"	9.3	12.23	2.39	6.8
ROUTH	"	9.14	12.34	2.49	6.19
TICKTON	"	9.25	12.45	3.0	6.30
HULL BRIDGE	"	9.32	12.52	3.7	6.37
BEVERLEY STN YARD	arr	9.45	1.5	3.20	6.50

OCTOBER 1903.

Beverley to Beeford Bus Service Timetable 1903

BRIDGES

The Bascule Bridge, Hull — Selby Railway. Carried the first railway to Hull in 1840.

Eppleworth Viaduct.
Hull & Barnsley

4-6-0 Schools Class No. 777 "Sir Lamiel" awaits the signal at Bridlington's platform one on a visit to the town in September 1982.

Ivatt 4MT simmers quietly ouside Bridlington shed.